IMPACT ATLANTA MAGAZINE

Vanessa M. Henderson
Editor-In-Chief

Terri Stephenson
Managing Editor

Susan Jones
Founder/Layout/Publisher

Rod Murphy
Photographer

Terri Robinson-Stephenson
Managing Editor

A Letter from the Publisher

Susan Jones, Founder

Hello beautiful people. I'm Susan Jones, a publisher and innovator that prepares and issues books, magazines and other media. There are many great publishers, to which I acknowledge. However, what sets me apart is my drive and my diverse capabilities in all aspects of business, which allow me to produce content that resonates with people from all walks of life. I am a writer, a think-er, a friend, a business woman and also a baker.

At Impact Atlanta Magazine International, we find that often in the media the bad and the ugly consume the headlines in Atlanta and cities like her. My goal with this maga-zine was and always will be to produce content that covers beauty while capturing culture, and highlighting positive stories that inspire and inform. My work won't be done until it leaves a lasting IMPACT.

Sincerely,

~Susan Jones

Contents

Where African Tradition Meets Fashion

Macintosh Smith (*Runway Photography*)   Francena Ottley (*in Studio Photography*)

Introducing
Vanessa Henderson
The Editor of
Impact Atlanta Magazine

Fashion designer Vanessa Henderson of Van Miller International, born June 7, 1958, in Reidsville, North Carolina, is known for her timeless designs, sophisticated knot dresses and couture aesthetic.

Vanessa was raised by a single mom and is the oldest of six siblings. Taught to sew by her mother, Vanessa learned to sew everything by hand. Married at seventeen years old she became a stay at home mother and began sewing for neighbors and friends for extra income. Once news spread throughout the small rural community orders became overwhelming. Vanessa continued to perfect her craft and decided to accept a job at a local fabric store as an Assistant Manager. Shortly after accepting the position Vanessa was presented with the opportunity to teach sewing at the local community college.

Designing has always been her life's passion. The thrill of educating students to pursue a career in fashion inspired her to continue to forge ahead and that's when she opened the doors to Vanessa's Bridal Image. Vanessa designed custom wedding gowns for the everyday bride. She quickly gained recognition for her cutting edge bridal looks in shades of every color.

 In 2001 Vanessa made the hard decision of leaving her roots behind and headed to Atlanta, Georgia to pursue her degree in Fashion Design from Bauder College. After graduating top of her class in 2003 Vanessa started Van Miller International and is now taking the fashion industry by storm with her trendsetting designs, couture opulence and comfortable yet edgy ready to wear ensembles. Featured in numerous publications, blogs, fashion shows and special events. Van Miller International is definitely a force to be reckoned with.

"Whether we have the means or not....we all, to some greater or lesser degree have an idea or a dream that we were created to achieve"   Vanessa Henderson~ Lady of the House"

Editoral

Feel the Impact

*O*h what a beautiful day it is. It seems like yesterday when Impact Atlanta was just a thought a dream. Today it is a reality. When I take a look back I'm filled with several emotions: excitement, happiness, love, anxiety and a host of others. But the feeling that rises above them all is accomplishment. The woman responsible for Impact has done it. The Impact staff has sacrificed and dedicated more than you could imagine making sure that our magazine, that our company is more than just a success in the industry. We are striving to become the template for the future of the fashion industry.

Atlanta has seen a lot of fashion. It truly has come full circle to be a major stop for the big box shows and events. The change continues to see the celebrity world become a big part. I feel that it is on the cusp of becoming a competitor to New York. Designers are making major strides in understanding, the ins and outs to get to the next level. The focus has changed the game, looks, trends, models, venues, play a major part

I hope this issue will enlighten you. We welcome your comments and suggestions with open arms. It is by you our readers we will perfect Impact Atlanta.

I thank you for your support and encouragement . So as you look through the pages we hope that you feel the Impact.

Vanessa M. Henderson
Editor-In-Chief

Legendary former
Harlem Globetrotter lead Showman
Matthew " Showbiz" Jackson!
Best Selling Co-Author for Anthology
"Soul Bearer" by Cheryl Polote-Williamson

Contact to schedule appearances,
speaking engagements,celebrity games etc.
and purchase your book copy today!
www.showbizjackson.com

Soul Bearer
Matthew Jackson
Co-Author

Shangani Fashion

Macintosh Smith (*Runway Photography*)   Francena Ottley (*in Studio Photography*)

Shangani Fashion designs are Juxtaposition of Culture and Style. Shangani is an African Tribe, named after its founder Shoshangani meaning "Traveler". Shangani Fashion is brand inspired by the travels and exposure to different cultural fashions of a Shangani designer and her desire to merge her travel experiences with ethnic and colorful prints to create a high fashion, ready-to-wear look. The traditional yet modern mix, is the passion behind Shangani Fashion design creations. The designs fit into all categories of fashion whether casual or formal for both men and women. Depending on the design and type of garment, the brand uses 100% dutch wax print, cotton, denim and blended materials of the finest quality. Completing the Afro-Inspired Look, Shangani Fashion also features handcrafted clutches, handbags, earrings, bracelets and shoes, adding a hint of sophistication to an individual's everyday look.

Shangani Fashion's debut presentation during New York Fashion Week conveys contemporary cuts that are accented with vintage accessories.

The design duo collaborating on the aesthetics is Fashion Designers Elesia Peterman and Mary Moore. Moore is a graduate of the University of Zimbabwe and a world traveler.

"My inspirations are fusions of my cultural, travel experiences and my Zimbabwean heritage and styles. Shoppers will find divers influences from the Caribbean, European and Middle-Eastern expressions in my fashions. I enjoy mixing various African influences with a contemporary cut and shape for a modernized look. And the result is a ready-to-wear brand that is suitable for all occasions" explains Mary Moore.

Shangani offers looks for both men and women, and intends to expand the menswear line for upcoming seasons. The garments are wearable for business casual or as formal wear. Depending on the type of garment design, the brand uses one-hundred percent cotton, applied with Dutch Wax print, Denim and other uniquely blended materials of the finest quality. Completing the Afro-inspired look, the Shangani brand also features handcrafted travel handbags and clutch bags. Accessories such as earrings, bracelets and shoes, add a hint of sophistication to an individual's look.

"My creative inspiration comes from a fusion of time, epoch periods and cultures, while remaining Afrocentric. "I want our line to show that African print transcends. The looks can be worn strictly as traditional wear, but the looks can also be incorporated in business and everyday casual use. What makes our line unique is that it isn't just an African meets Western cohesion. Our goal is to reach and inspire a much bigger market. Our line is an international fusion. Also, being a millennial, I feel I can relate with the style trends my peers are excited about..

I want to use clothing design as my voice and demonstration of creativity."

~Elesia Peterman.

Lupus
The Purple Group
Bringing Awareness to LUPUS

Who Gets Lupus?
Anyone can get lupus, but it most often affects women. Lupus is also more common in women of African American, Hispanic, Asian, and Native American descent than in Caucasian women.

What Causes Lupus?
The cause of lupus is not known. Research suggests that genes play an important role, but genes alone do not determine who gets lupus. It is likely that many factors trigger the disease.

What Are the Symptoms of Lupus?
Symptoms of lupus vary, but some of the most common symptoms of lupus are:

- Pain or swelling in joints
- Muscle pain
- Fever with no known cause
- Red rashes, most often on the face
- Chest pain when taking a deep breath
- Hair loss
- Pale or purple fingers or toes
- Sensitivity to the sun
- Swelling in legs or around eyes
- Mouth ulcers
- Swollen glands
- Feeling very tired.

Less common symptoms include:

- Anemia (a decrease in red blood cells)
- Headaches
- Dizzy spells
- Feeling sad
- Confusion
- Seizures.

Symptoms may come and go. The times when a person is having symptoms are called flares, which can range from mild to severe. New symptoms may appear at any time.

How Is Lupus Diagnosed?
There is no single test to diagnose lupus. It may take months or years for a doctor to diagnose lupus. Your doctor may use many tools to make a diagnosis:

- Medical history
- Complete exam
- Blood tests
- Skin biopsy (looking at skin samples under a microscope
- Kidney biopsy (looking at tissue from your kidney under a microscope).

How Is Lupus Treated?
You may need special kinds of doctors to treat the many symptoms of lupus. Your health care team may include:

- A family doctor
- Rheumatologists—doctors who treat arthritis and other diseases that cause swelling in the joints
- Clinical immunologists—doctors who treat immune system disorders
- Nephrologists—doctors who treat kidney disease
- Hematologists—doctors who treat blood disorders
- Dermatologists—doctors who treat skin diseases
- Neurologists—doctors who treat problems with the nervous system
- Cardiologists—doctors who treat heart and blood vessel problems
- Endocrinologists—doctors who treat problems related to the glands and hormones
- Nurses
- Psychologists

The Purple Group

Alex Johnson   Yan Li,   Terrasea Page,   Rachel Nadia

Hair: Shaquille Butler   Make-up: Shonett Hill & Mercedes Jackson   Black Tie Photography

Black Tie Photography

Black Tie Photography

BLACKOUT

MY 40 YEARS IN THE MUSIC BUSINESS

PAUL PORTER

PAUL PORTER

by JoHonda F. Rogers

IDM: This is your first book. What made you decide to write *Blackout*?

Paul: I've always believe that our stories should be shared. The music-business has been my life. A chosen few get to experience how it actually works. "Blackout" allows you to candidly take a critical look.

IDM: Why did you choose the title *Blackout*?

Paul: Blackout has several meanings, and all of them are appropriate.

IDM: How do you think the radio industry will respond to this book?

Paul: I actually don't care. The most important thing for me was to tell the story.

IDM: What did you find the hardest to write about in the book?

Paul: The story for me was easy. I found comfort in telling my story.

IDM: Do you think "Pay to Play" is still an issue with American radio in 2017?

Paul: "Pay for Play" will never end. Capitalism runs the culture. To expect anything less would be un-American.

IDM: Some may say you wrote this book for revenge. What are your thoughts on this subject?

Paul: You've got jokes. Who would I be getting even with? I've been shaking off haters for decades.

IDM: How are the playlists at your station, The Wire, created?

Paul: I select every song on our playlist. Using my ears, research, statistics, should be the barometer of any radio station. Unfortunately, pay for play, has replaced ears, with money.

IDM: What are your predictions for the future of the music industry as far as radio is concerned?

Paul: Radio is always going to survive. While steaming, and the internet will allow a greater selection, I personally think that local content counts.

IDM: What are you most excited for readers to learn more about from reading *Blackout*?

Paul: Blackout, is a inside look at the industry from a insiders perspective. I've been blessed to work, at and with some of the industries biggest players and times. I have been a lifetime student of the game. And more importantly, I have no fear or restraints on telling the truth.

IDM: Do you have any plans to write something similar to *Blackout* in the future?

Paul: For now, I think this story is more than enough. I do want to do a documentary for the big screen.

DETROIT'S OWN
KEVIN CARTER
ARTISTRY OF HAIR

KEVIN CARTER
HAIR EXTRAORDINAIRE!

KEVIN CARTER, owner of **ARTISTRY OF HAIR SALON**, "Where Hair & Art Come Together,"

in Farmington Hills, Michigan, is a master stylist, educator, innovator, competition fantasy hair designer and mentor to up-and-coming stylists. For more than three decades, Kevin has entertained audiences around the world with his extraordinary fantasy avant-garde hair creations. Kevin's reputation precedes him as one of the industry leaders in showcasing innovative techniques and hair artistry. He has competed and won multiple trophies and first place honors throughout his career. Some of his victories include the Bronner Brother's International Battle Royale, Wolverine State Cosmetologist Association competition, the Proud Lady World Class Fantasy Competition, International Fantasy Hair Competition (New Hampshire), Hair Ballers, Golden Scissors and Hair Wars.

Kevin has trained cosmetologists at Dudley's Cosmetology University, The Beauty Culture League, Breithaupt Career Center, Oakland Technical Schools, and Virginia Ferrell Cosmetology School, as well as those whom he has taken under his wing throughout his career. Kevin's extraordinary hair creations have been featured in several well-known media including:

Print *Detroit Metro Times, Hour Detroit, W, Sophisticated Black Hair, Time Magazine, Fantasy, Black Passion and American Salon magazines, and the book, "Hair Wars"*

by Johanna Lenander
Stage *"The Hair Show," starring Chaka Khan*
Television *Dateline NBC*
Silver Screen *"Good Hair," narrated by Chris Rock*
Kevin's mission as a cosmetologist has always been to continually exceed expectations in the hair and beauty industry, by working together with industry professionals to train up-and-coming stylists to keep Detroit as the **Hair Capital of the World**. Currently, Kevin and his team of professionals are preparing for the fifth Annual Artistry of Hair and Fashion Show to be held Sunday, April 30, 2017, 4:00pm at St. Johns Banquet and Conference Center in Southfield, Michigan.

KEVIN SHARES A FEW FACTS

IDM: How did you get started and why the name Artistry of Hair.

KEVIN: I got started in cosmetology from finger waving my hair in my high school years. I was always talented in art so the more creative the hair designs became Artistry of Hair just seem right for the name.

IDM: How long have you been in the hair industry and where do you see yourself in the ext five years.

KEVIN: I have been in the hair industry for 33 years. I see myself in the next 5 years opening a cosmetology school, and dev eloping a product line.

IDM: What do you feel is your greatest accomplishment. What would be your advice to the up and coming stylist in the industry.

KEVIN: My greatest accomplishment is being able to give back to others. My advice to up and coming cosmetologist would be to practice your craft and be as professional as possible.

IDM: If you could show your Art any where in the world where would it be and what would be your theme.

KEVIN: If I could show my art anywhere in the world it would be the Smithsonian, Titled: Artistry of Hair.

IDM: How many years have you been doing this show and why did you want to do it?

KEVIN: I have been doing the Artistry of Hair & Fashion Show for 5 years. I want to continue the show because it helps raise the bar for seasoned and up and coming professionals.

SUBSCRIBE TODAY
WWW.FAITHMAGAZINE.COM
IMPACTDETROITMAG.COM

Met Gala Piece by
O'Neal Wyche

Model Spotlight

Cynasure Renae

I am Cynasure Renae, of Pontiac, Michigan, and a curvy model working in the commercial runway and print segments of fashion. This name is derived from the Latin and French word *cynosure* meaning "a person or thing that is the center of attention or admiration." I have maintained keen interest in modeling since watching my Delta Sigma Theta grandmother at sorority banquets and fashion shows. My very first runway show was in high school and my second show, during college at the University of Michigan, was also my first tear sheet feature in Noir Magazine.

My modeling experience thus far has taken place in Detroit and New York. I have been featured in publications such as Fashionatra the Fashion Blog and SDM Live Magazinc. I have done runway in custom and boutique fashions for WALK Fashion Show Detroit, Walk Fashion Show NYFW and Dream Runway Show, among many others. I have completed my first print project last year in a calendar production, Bigsexzfromthedcalendarfirstedition. My most recent runway events were Kiss My Curves by The Fashion Statement, an all curvy production and the Kevin Carter Artistry of Fashion Show.

I also have experience in runway training and backstage runway show production. Likewise, I am very social and I have accomplished production and hostess capacities of Detroit Gatsby events and Detroit Social Connection events. There's always a fashion opportunity! I feel empowered by my aspirations most when I am approached by an individual that recognizes me from a runway show. I am amazed when people comment on how I inspired them with my confidence and poise. I believe in never telling yourself no and wearing your joy. I am 'the' next designer's muse. IG:@lacoxanoxtra

ATLANTA'S OWN FEARLESS
TINA FEARS
RISING STAR

"Be strong and courageous. The Lord God will be with you where ever you go"
~ Joshua 1:9

I'm excited to have a candid conversation with the fabulous and FEARLESS Tina Fears. I'll just begin by looking unto God and acknowledging the amazing things that he does in our lives everyday. I've watched him show up when I didn't see a way out. God brings people in your life that you can admire and see him through them. People of faith are walking in victory! Let's get this conversation started!

~ Terri Robinson Stephenson

TINA FEARS

IDM: Tina, we have been following your career for a number of years now. Please tell us how you got into the entertainment industry?

Tina: Ok, well, thank you so much to Impact Detroit Magazine for even taking an interest in my journey. I come from an entertainment family. Both of my parents were involved in the entertainment community in Los Angeles. So, I've been around music my entire life. As a little girl, I remember me and my sister going with both of my parents and being able to sit in the studios with a lot of different songwriters and different artists, and my sister and I having to be quiet on the sofa while my dad laid down tracks. So, unlike a lot of people who took an interest in entertainment, I feel like I was someone who was born into it. Music was always around me. It's a part of my home. If my mom was not singing or working with my dad, she was always handling other side of the business. Entertainment is something that is a part of my DNA.

IDM: Tina, not only are you a phenomenal vocalist, actress, dancer, choreographer and entertainer. I understand that you are also an Entrepreneur, having started your own successful business with what I've been told was "fifty dollars and a vision." Tell us about that Stage Ready vision.

Tina: Ok, I actually started my company Stage Ready with what I'll call $100 and a dream. Basically, I only had one hundred dollars a n d a d r e a m . M y company, Stage Ready, is something that I created as a way to use my natural God-given talents to make a living. I went to C l a r k A t l a n t a University, with goals of becoming an educator. But, when you're called to do something the Lord has a way of bringing you back around to what He calls you to do. So, after leaving Clark Atlanta, I still knew that I had a really special call on my life. And instead of doing what was safe, I decided to take a leap of faith and use my natural God given talents as an artist and my business savviness, which the talented component of me is from my dad, and the business savviness is from my mother, so I started my own company, Stage Ready. The vision behind Stage Ready was to originally

TINA FEARS

change the face of the faith-based industry. Back when I started Stage Ready, in the early 2000's. I would see shows like Video Gospel see what was considered to be contemporary gospel, but I felt like it was very under represented. The music videos were really cheesy, a lot of the artists were not dressed in a way that was relevant even though they were calling themselves contemporary Christian artists. So, I made it my personal goal to change it, I love the Lord, and my faith is very important to me, so I partnered my beliefs with my passion for entertainment and it helped change the face of the gospel industry So, Stage Ready, and our focus at the time was choreography, creative direction and artist development. The original focus, was to use the old Motown formula of developing artists from start to finish, whether it be through styling hair, makeup, obviously choreography, and just helping to put shows together. This again was to help change the face of the gospel industry. Because you had people who were, Kirk Franklin, and One Nation, and people like Tonex and Dietrick Haddon, and people like that who were doing ground-breaking things, and things that the gospel industry wasn't ready for. They were way ahead of their time, but it was something that younger believers could relate to because they dresse d stylishly, and when Mary Mary came out with the micro-braids, and all the color in their hair, it spoke to the time. And so Stage Ready has evolved over the past 10 years, and we've been very blessed to work with people like Smokey Norful and Deitrick Haddon, We've shared concert billing with Tye Tribett, Tonex and Mary Mary, The list goes on. But, I do feel like now, looking back, that I was able to make an impact because of a lot of the things I was able to do with those artists, whether it be putting together their celebration of gospel performances, working with Dietrich for many years with his tours, and, helping him write songs, and contributing my gifts in the creative direction with him and his team. Those people kind of paved the way for the next groups we see. So, when we see people like Tasha Cobbs and her styling team, and we see people like Tye with his singers, ~ continued

TINA FEARS

you know, dressing and preparing for the show, those are things that 10 years ago, some of the artists that I was blessed to work with, started doing. Creating looks before they get on stage, thinking about putting a show together.

IDM: I understand that you have also been recognized by the City of Atlanta and Mayor Kaseem Reid as one of the most successful Black Entrepreneurs under 30. Tell us about that experience, and how did that come about ?

Tina: I was honored to be selected as a finalist for a magazine called "Under 30" following the Vision, and at the time this was a group of young entrepreneurs that were all under the ages of 30 that had different businesses. Some people were writers, other people had vintage boutiques, one lady started her own hair care product line. So, it was a spotlight on young individuals, that weren't 30 yet, who were really breaking the ground and blazing a trail for themselves. It was wonderful because I was part of the inaugural edition, which was endorsed by Mayor Kaseem Reid, It was really a blessing because I was honored among many people who were peers of mine, though we were in different industries. I've seen them climb the ladder of success. And many are still in business today. Some of us have evolved from that time we were honored, but I feel like that will be something that will always be a part of my journey as a businesswoman, and that's something I'm very thankful for.

IDM: Tina, as creative director for USHER'S New Look, Celebration of Gospel, Smokie Norful, Melonie Fiona, TALIAH WAAJID'S Annual International Natural Hair Shows, held in both Atlanta, GA and New York, NY; a leading role as Michelle in the Stage Play Dream Girls and several other musical stage plays to

your credit; having toured with Detroit's own Gospel Artist Deitrick Haddon; and, I understand that you were even the featured vocalist on the Grammy Nominated "Walking on Water" recorded by gospel Artist Lacrea… How do you balance your family life?

Tina: Wow! That's a lot, I don't really think about it until someone says it out, and when I hear that, it reminds me of the different seasons I was in, in my life when I was doing each of those projects. I'm very grateful to my amazing husband, Martin Fears, who is my sweetheart, my support, my silent partner. And of course our son, Micah Isaiah Fears, who is six. Now, how do I balance it all? I really take it one day at a time. I have a support system with my mother, my sister, my in-laws, my sisters-in-law. And we just try to make it happen. There are times when, we always say, " It takes a village." There are times when I have to be on set and I have to take my son to my sister and my husband picks him up. We just juggle it all. But, it's a blessing to be able to pursue my dreams and know that I have a support system that believes in what I'm doing. And when I take on each project, no matter how challenging it is, I feel like I'm representing my whole tribe when I do it, so it just pushes me to really do my absolute best. So, I guess I don't have an exact answer for you, and I'm not really sure how I do it sometimes. Definitely lots of prayer, and I probably should rest more than I do. But really, I could not do it without the support system of my family. And when everything is done, I try to take a break like a vacation, or I go to the spa, and just rest and reflect so I can be prepared to get back out there when the next opportunity presents itself. ~ continued

TINA FEARS

IDM: As a young Black female, what have been some of your challenges, if any, breaking into this industry?

Tina: I think that's a really great question, because when I think back to being a preteen, singing and dancing always came naturally. But because I was so much around the arts, I never really had the dream that I was going to be a star one day. I just knew that I had a special set of gifts, and I knew that in some kind of way I was going to do something with them. As I've gotten older, I've become braver, and I found myself becoming more fearless as I approach each thing. So, I guess the challenges of breaking into the entertainment industry, or any industry, is overcoming your fear and then finding your niche. Sometimes, we can just find ourselves searching or trying to figure out what's going to stick. I'm someone who's multi-talented, so I do a lot of different things, so I think once you find out what your niche is, you just have to be fearless and pursue what those things are. For example, if someone said they wanted to be a model. I think it's one thing to want to do it, but it's another thing when you have a

gift to do something. And once you realize that you have a gift, you just have to be fearless in attacking and pursuing it by any means necessary. So, when you're trying to find opportunities, or figuring out something that's worth doing, for free, and figuring out when it's time to be honest before you give, that can be a challenge sometimes. And sometimes, I'll be transparent because I hope that my feedback can be a blessing to someone. There are a lot of challenges. I live in Atlanta, so the market is very saturated. Whether you are a dancer, a writer, or an actor, there's a lot going on in Atlanta right now. Sometimes, because there are limited opportunities, you'll find the same 25 people going after one job. You see the same people auditioning at the same time, you see the same people at open calls, so that can be very discouraging. But when you know God has something specifically for you, you just have to continue to pursue it by any means necessary, and then when you feel like you're hitting a road block, you just gotta step back and evaluate, and kinda change your focus up a little bit, then jump back out there and get it. ~ continued

TINA FEARS

TINA FEARS

IDM: As a dancer, choreographer, and vocalist, are you're formally trained? Or just a God blessed gift?

Tina: That's another great question, I am not classically or formally trained in any of the things I do professionally. I'm not a prima, I didn't, study ballet, I didn't study with any world-renowned vocal coaches; my dad was my vocal coach. We sang from the time we could talk, and that has been a gift, and has been a curse sometimes. In musical theater, you get what's called libretto, and that's speaking to some of the stage plays and musicals that I've done. So libretto is basically the whole show on sheet music. Because I didn't go to a performing arts school I'm just flowing on the natural ability. I have to rely on my ear heavily, which can be a challenge during music week, because everyone is reading straight from sheet music and I had to wait for the keys to be powered before I could hear what it is. On the flip side, some people, once you take the sheet music away, they can't sing it unless they've got the music in front of them, whereas I can rely on my natural ability and my ear to hear and retain the information. The same thing goes for choreography; I move well, I was always an athlete growing up, so that helps, but to answer your question, I'm flowing straight off of God's anointing and just the gift that he has given me. You know, it's polished out through the years, just doing shows and going through the process you always get better, and, hopefully again I inspire somebody else because I do believe that training and education are very important if you're blessed with that, but just because you don't have that set of tools doesn't mean that you can't offer something, especially when it's a gift.

IDM: I have a little-known fact Ms. Fabulous Fears; I heard you are also known to some in the industry as "FaBu." Where did that name come from?

Tina: Ha, that's so funny. That is a nickname from when I was in the dance department at "Usher's New Look," which is Usher's foundation for youth. It's his non-profit, and back in the early 2000s that foundation had what was like a fame camp. They had music, arts, sports, dance, and acting. I was on the dance component, and so all the camp counselors, my peers actually gave me the name "FaBu." it was short for Fabulous, and it just kind of stuck around during the camp, and even now, you know, I run into some of the students who are now adults that went to the camp and they still call me "FaBu." So that was like my nickname from Usher's Camp New Look.

IDM: Tina, is there anything you would like our readers to know about you that we have not covered here today?

Tina: I have some really exciting things that are coming up. I have been blessed with the opportunity to play "*Nina # Three*" in a show called "Simply Simone" here in Atlanta, and it's a celebration of the music and life of the legendary Nina Simone. It's not a biographical show, where we're, telling the story of her life in chronological order; none of us are playing Nina Simone, but instead we represent her at different times in her life, kind of as we tell her story through music. There are only four women in the show and I'm one of them, and the show is playing at *"TheTheatrical Outfit"* in Atlanta, and so, because I'm someone that sings with a lower register, to be able to get an opportunity to sing something by Nina Simone is just like a once in a lifetime Opportunity. It starts March 23rd and closes April 15th in Atlanta, so depending on when this article comes out, you can decide on how relevant that is, but you may say it in the past tense. It is a lot of hard work and

~ continued

Production photography by Christopher Bartelski

(Clockwise) Tina Fears, Chelsea Reynolds, Chani Maisonet and Marliss Amiea

(Left To Right) Chani Maisonet, Marliss Amiea, Chelsea Reynolds and Tina Fears

very challenging, so I'm excited to be a part of it and just wanna go and do my best every single day. I'm actually in rehearsals now, so even talking about it makes me a little nervous because we have a very long way to go in a very short period of time, but it's a blessing to be a part of the participating show.

Also, in September of 2016 I was cast as a principal in a commercial for Ford Motor Company. They have a new campaign called "Born to be Bold" that basically captures the life of three women of color; one is a dancer, one is a chef, and one is a pilot. It captures us in our element, and shows how women like us drive Fords. So, in addition to being in the commercial, I was also able to do voice overs for that commercial as well. That's just, I mean, coming full circle; a little girl from L.A. who started a business in the entertainment industry and has gone on to do shows and land a commercial with one of the biggest brands in the world is just like, I'm in awe of what God can do, and I'm very excited about things to come. I'm also going to be making a small

appearance on *Green Leaf,* which is a show that's on, The *OWN* network so I'll be on one of the episodes for that as well. Just trying to, you know, stay busy and just be available to the Lord and see what opportunities open up from here.

IDM: As I conclude, what would you say to any young Black female that has the aspiration to dream, or even have a vision, yet are afraid to step out on faith? What would you want her to take away from this very candid interview?

Tina: I mentioned earlier about the importance of being fearless, and that's something that is a mantra for me; it's my life's motto. Obstacles happen, things happen that are beyond our control, some things we can't change. We can try to run away from stuff, hide, but you know you can't get away from it, but I think that as long as you have hope, that at the end of the day as long as I have an opportunity to get up and try again, then I'm fearless with it. It could be the simplest task, you know, like, I'm going to graduate

from high school. Life may be crazy, my family situation may be crazy, but I'm determined to graduate from high school. Or you know what? I want to be a cosmetologist. I'm going to go to hair school if I have to work three jobs to do it. If that individual is fearless, and their approach is to be diligent, it can happen. So, if I am speaking to dreamers right now, what's the worst that can happen if you fail? You fail, what do you do? You get up and you attack it again. So, for someone who has been knocked down, and someone who has seen obstacles and has been through really rough times, there's always, a light at the end of the tunnel. So, I just want to encourage people to keep hoping and keep dreaming; if you get an idea, it's not by accident, because you have something really awesome to contribute to the world. If you keep moving by faith and are filled with it, you never know what can happen if you don't try. Amen. Thank you, thank you so much.

IDM: Thank you for sharing your amazing story.

-END

Photographer Elvis Piedra

GALLERY

Black Tie Photography

Photographer Sammy Saxon

VAN MILLER
INTERNATIONAL

Black Tie Photography

Black Tie Photography

Black Tie Photography

Photographer Rodrick Murphy

Photographer Rodrick Murphy

Photographer Rodrick Murp

Photographer Rodrick Murphy

Photographer Rodrick Murphy

Photographer Rodrick Murphy

Photographer Rodrick Murphy

Photographer Rodrick Murphy

Photographer Rodrick Murphy

Photographer Rodrick Murphy

Photographer Rodrick Murphy

Photographer Rodrick Murphy

Photographer Rodrick Murphy